PARENTING TEENAGERS FOR EMOTIONAL STABILITY

Raising Adolescent with A Balanced Emotion

By

LAUREL TAYLOR

COPYRIGHT

Copyright © (Laurel Taylor) 2023. All rights reserved

DISCLAIMER

This book is only intended to provide knowledge that is relevant to daily life. Every effort has been made to provide accurate, current, trustworthy and comprehensive information. Consult your therapist for guidance and counselling.

CONTENTS

Introduction

The teenage years in children can be some of the most difficult times in their lives, as any parent would know or at least have been warned. If their parents are divorcing or living apart, it may be especially difficult.

Any parent may find it difficult to deal with the fast-paced effects of puberty, hormones, high school, and the rising yearning for independence. Every day might feel like a struggle in a family with a teenager, often over the most trivial of issues. As a parent, you want to be able to love and discipline your child the same way you always have, but you also need to realize that as your child changes, so does your relationship with them. It's beneficial for kids to know that their parents are there for them and are willing to recognize that they have a young adult who requires their respect and advice because these are some of the most formative years of their lives.

Adolescence brings with it a new struggle for independence, as well as more time spent with peers and less time with family. Teenagers start to feel less emotionally reliant on their parents, although this emotional independence frequently develops after a time of conflict and heightened negative emotional experience. Early adolescents frequently have greater negative affect than younger children, but during high school, the negative effect frequently lessens. But, compared to males, girls frequently suffer a long time of high negative impact. Even in response to the same occurrence, adolescents frequently exhibit more strong emotions than their parents, both good and negative.

Early adolescence is characterized by an increase in unpleasant emotional experiences that coincides with the development of abstract thought. Adolescents frequently look for a solid peer group as the backdrop for emotional regulation as they struggle with social issues that are more abstract and complex. The acceptance of equality and the propensity to provide emotional support lead to the development of positive peer relationships. Teenagers who are not accepted by their peers run the danger of engaging in criminal activity and dropping out of school. In the peer setting of adolescence, even teenagers who are accepted by their peers and have close friends frequently display an increase in negative emotions like anger and anxiety. Generally, adolescent peer relationships that are helpful and good foster healthy emotional growth and mental health as the adolescent transitions into adulthood.

The prevalence of dating relationships increases during adolescence, although young adolescents may still struggle to comprehend how one person can elicit conflicting and divergent emotions. Because of this, adolescent dating is frequently marked by a wide range of emotions. Dating partners are equally prone to feeling envious, especially if they misjudge their partner's intentions while interpreting their acts.

On their transition to adulthood, teenagers need to create their identities. Teenagers and young adults frequently experience significant levels of anxiety while examining a wide range of identity alternatives, yet they still seem interested in doing so. Teenagers who commit to an identity early on—typically an identity that is supported by their family—had low levels of anxiety and rarely have problems with their parents. Teenagers who are not considering their identity possibilities frequently have low levels of motivation and seem bored or disinterested. They have worse peer interactions and are most vulnerable to mental health issues as adults. Last but not least, young adults who have developed a solid sense of who they often have a greater capacity for empathy and emotional control.

Chapter 1

Understanding the Emotional Health of Your Adolescent

A time of transition from childhood to maturity is the adolescent years. Teenagers frequently have a strong urge to live independently. They could struggle as a result of still depending on their parents. Teens may feel overpowered as a result of the emotional and physical changes they experience.

Other pressures that teens could experience include:
- blending in with friends and in school
- achieving academic success and receiving good grades
- excelling in sports and other activities
- participating as a family member
- part-time employment is held
- in preparing for their post-high school life, whether it be college or something else

The teenage years are crucial as your child establishes their unique identity. Many parents are unsure about what they can do to support their adolescents.

A Way to Better Health

The most crucial thing you can do to support your child during their adolescent years is to express your affection for them. The way that children are treated by their parents greatly influences how they feel about themselves. Parents must give their kids self-confidence for this reason. This is possible by:

- enhancing their self-worth and assurance.
- give them praise, and be precise. Describe your admiration or pride for them in detail. Spend time with them and express your appreciation for them.
- giving them emotional support.
- invite them to communicate with you. Help them out by being receptive to their feelings.
- ensuring their security and safety.

- offer them your undivided affection. Keep the same routines so they feel safe. Assure them that their house is a safe place.
- by instilling in their resilience.
- teach your youngster how to survive difficult situations. Assist them in managing stress, adjusting to change, and recovering from failures.

Communicating your values to your child is also crucial. Establish boundaries and expectations for them. Insisting on honesty, restraint, and respect for others at all times are a few examples of these. Let your adolescent be themselves while also giving them their own space.

Teenage parents typically learn that their children only notice the problems. They can start to offer mainly unfavorable feedback as a pattern. Teens need criticism, but encouragement works better with them. Remember to commend appropriate behavior. Your teen will feel accomplished as a result, and your family's values will be strengthened.

Building a caring bond from the beginning will support you and your child as they navigate the challenging teenage years.

Parents can get ready for their child's adolescent years in the following ways:

1. Provide a loving and secure home atmosphere.
2. Establish an environment of integrity, respect, and trust.
3. Permit boldness and independence that are age-appropriate.
4. Establish a bond with your teen that will motivate them to confide in you when they are distressed.
5. Educate your teen to be accountable for their own and your possessions.
6. Teach your children fundamental responsibility for housework.
7. Instill the value of accepting limitations.
8. Remember how important rules are. Rules affecting their health, safety, and education are still necessary for teens. Make rules

simple to comprehend. When you establish a rule, make sure the justifications are obvious.

9. Pay attention to your child's requests, thoughts, and worries. Make a compromise if you can.

Something to Think About

Keep in mind that as your kid attempts to define himself or herself, they may explore. They might alter their beliefs, morals, appearance, hairdo, or attire to achieve this. This is typical conduct. You have nothing to worry about. On the other hand, inappropriate or harmful behavior might indicate a problem.

Some teenagers are more likely to engage in certain self-destructive behaviors. These teenagers frequently suffer from low self-esteem or familial issues. They might experiment with drinking, taking drugs, or engaging in unprotected intercourse. Some prevalent health problems affecting teenagers include eating disorders and depression. The indications that your child may be having issues include the ones listed below:

1. uneasy or agitated behavior
2. gain or loss of weight
3. decline in grades
4. difficulty concentrating
5. always feeling depressed
6. disregard towards others and things
7. a lack of drive
8. loss of interest in activities, exhaustion, and energy
9. a low sense of self
10. difficulty falling asleep
11. encounters with the law

What Should I Do If An Issue Arises?

Cooperate to keep lines of communication open. Ask your teen about their concerns if you think there may be an issue. To make a problem go away, don't ignore it. When issues are minor, they are simpler to handle. This allows you and your teen the chance to practice problem-solving techniques together. Never hesitate to seek assistance when managing your teen.

Questions Parents Frequently Ask

1. What can I do to maintain my adolescent's emotional stability?
2. Is my adolescent's behavior typical?
3. What indications should I look for if I believe my adolescent may be experiencing issues?
4. I suffer from depression and low self-esteem. Is there a higher chance that my child may experience those issues?
5. Should I take my adolescent to a therapist or a psychiatrist?
6. Does my adolescent need medication?
7. Will these habits "grow out" of my adolescence?"

Chapter 2

How to Handle Teens Emotions

Adolescent life isn't shown in movies. Trying to combine school, schoolwork, your family, and your social life is tough. Trauma and drama must also be dealt with.

You're irritated and frustrated, whether your best buddy cancels plans to spend more time with the latest shiny product or someone is spreading false information about you online. It's possible that you feel pressure to perform better than everyone else to protect "your future," and this pressure is making you so stressed that you're missing sleep and changing your weight.

How can you get better when everyone around you in adolescence seems to be experiencing the thrill and possibilities of teen life except for you? There must be a method to manage this emotional roller coaster. Here are some do's and don'ts to be mindful about.

Do's

1. Take charge of your feelings?

Are you insane? Angry? Sad? Frustrated? By recognizing your feelings, you can take control of your emotions.BIt lessens the intensity of such feelings to put them into words.

2. It helps you to escape your mind

Emotions can run their natural course when you take the time to identify what you are feeling. Knowing the feeling makes it easier to experience relief from it.

3. It is a practice of mindfulness.

You must identify your feelings to express them verbally. You can undertake some self-reflection while you're quiet thanks to this mindfulness practice.

4. Eliminates your uncertainty.

We frequently misunderstand how we feel bad. We have a feeling, but we're not sure what it is. As you name your emotions, you not only start to comprehend what is upsetting you but also start to comprehend how you are feeling about it. You may feel better as a result of that acceptance and clarity.

5. Take up surfing

You must acquire the skill of "riding the wave of emotion," which is a dialectical behavior therapy technique.

This is how it goes. When we're sad, it's easy to get mired in the details, and believes that by thinking about it, we can make the emotion go away. Nonetheless, this may lead to us becoming mired in unfavorable mental patterns. To allow emotions to develop naturally, we must instead leave the loop and enter them.

6. Get it out of your system in a healthy way. Trying to suppress or ignore your emotions can only make matters worse. You shouldn't dismiss the message that your emotions are trying to convey to you. Even if suppressing those sensations temporarily makes you feel better, you

will still be experiencing those emotions. Stomach aches or worse can result from holding in your emotions.

It's healthy for you, so get it out of your system while you can! In particular, weeping causes your body to release endorphins and the "feel-good" hormone oxytocin. Your mental and bodily suffering is lessened by them. A nice weep will make you feel better.

Here are some alternative methods of crying that you can try:
- Exercise. You can skateboard, ride a bike, run, surf, box, lift weights, or engage in any other activity that will help you let go of those endorphins and stored energy.
- Play your favorite music as you go. Your mood can be lifted by dancing, having fun, and engaging in activities like karaoke.
- Engage in a hobby you enjoy. Making fun videos for social media, engaging in a sport, fidgeting with a hobby, or playing a

game (for a while!) can all help you remember the happy times and move on.

- Unwind. A soothing activity might offer you some time to think through — and get past — your sentiments, whether it's taking a bath, baking, or even cleaning.

7. Get in touch

Nobody can successfully navigate life on their own. Now and then, we could all use some help. It is not a show of weakness to reach out to a friend or family member. It's a sign of strength, emotional intelligence, and self-assurance. It's the aspect of "adulting" that even many people still struggle with. Your stress can be reduced by talking to someone. Also, it can help you feel better when someone acknowledges how you're feeling and validates it. Having a conversation with a friend, a member of your family, or a therapist might also help you gain perspective. That person will frequently even assist you in coming up with answers to your problems.

The benefits of therapy make therapists the best choice. As long as you don't indicate any imminent risk to yourself or others, therapists are required by law to keep all information confidential and not disclose it to your parents or anyone else.

Don'ts

1. Avoid Posting on Social

When you post on social media when you're depressed or furious, things frequently get worse. Strong feelings can cause you to write something you'll later regret. Also, depending on your level of rage, your post can constitute cyberbullying.

Negatively utilizing social media won't improve your mood. However, it might seriously harm your future once it has been placed online. Even after deletion, it still exists. This can have an impact on your possible connections in the future or even a job.

2. Having an instantaneous response

A hasty response will likely make you regret it as well. It's crucial to settle down and sit with your emotions. It is a recipe for disaster to impulsively say or do something to the person who upset you (even if that person is you!). Without pausing to consider your actions, you might experience the following:

- humiliated by what you said or did
- guilty of injuring the other person
- irate with yourself for making things worse rather than better

However, retaliating harshly could harm your reputation.

3. The hand that feeds you, bite

Think carefully before responding to someone who offers to assist you. Whether it's a parent, a sibling, a friend, a coach, a teacher, or anyone else. They must care about you if they are offering to assist. They will probably comply if you yell at them or tell them to leave you alone in your response.

What's worse, they might remember how you answered and decide not to assist you when you ask them for a recommendation letter or ask your parent for money. If you don't want their assistance, say so politely but emphatically. Tell them you need to solve this problem on your own and thank them for their offer.

4. Self-punish yourself

Hurting yourself won't make your problems go away. Self-harm is merely a short-term release, whether you're starving yourself, cutting or burning your skin, bingeing, and purging, or engaging in any other destructive behavior. While it may feel nice for a moment to manage your emotional anguish, doing so won't help you resolve your problems. Self-harm can also develop into a habit or turn into something far worse.

In conclusion, there are constructive and destructive approaches to managing your emotions. The wholesome ones will assist you in moving on. The toxic relationships will make you regret them.

Determine what it is you are truly feeling, allow yourself to feel it, accept it, pick a healthy outlet for it, practice self-care, and be open to assistance.

Chapter 3

Why It's Crucial to Recognize and Control Your Emotions

The development and wellness of children and adolescents depend on their ability to understand and control their emotions. Being able to comprehend and control one's emotions increases a person's likelihood such that when you feel powerful emotions like disappointment, irritation, or enthusiasm, you express them by speaking quietly or in acceptable ways. In other words, they act in a way that doesn't harm other people, things, or themselves. Controlled impulses behave in this way.

And this is advantageous for kids since it promotes their learning, socialization, independence, and other positive outcomes. It takes time for your child to learn how to comprehend and control their emotions. The ability to recognize emotions will require assistance for your child. This primarily entails identifying and labeling feelings, which builds the foundation for managing emotions as your child becomes older. Other techniques for controlling emotions independently will become more apparent to your child as they get older.

Emotional regulation is the process of understanding and controlling emotions. Your child's ability to self-regulate depends on it.

Strengthening Emotional Competencies In Preteens And Teenagers

Teenagers and preteens frequently experience intense, sometimes paralyzing feelings like embarrassment and shame. Even though adolescents may be familiar with the names of these feelings, when distressed they nevertheless struggle to identify them. Teenagers can lack the ability to express and manage their emotions in an adult manner due to the way their brains develop during adolescence.

Preadolescents and adolescents still require assistance in understanding and controlling their emotions. Your child will become more adept at controlling their emotions on their own with time and effort.

The following tips can help your child become more adept at comprehending and controlling their emotions as they enter their teenage years:

1. If you notice feelings beginning to erupt, take action. Your child will find it simpler to maintain control of their behavior if they can recognize their emotional changes as soon as possible.

2. Encourage your child to identify the early bodily indicators of intense emotions. For instance, "Lately, when I was detained in traffic, my heart was pounding and I felt quite heated." When you're angry, does that happen to you?

3. Encourage your kid to recognize early behavioral indications of intense emotions. Have a discussion with your child about what you do if you see the beginnings of

powerful emotions. For instance, "When I begin to feel particularly irritated with myself, I instead focus on something I'm proud of." Do you think that would work?

4. Together, create a list of activities your child could do, such as going for a run, putting on headphones and listening to loud music, or practicing meditation, when they feel intense emotions starting to rise. So that your child can select options that feel good in various circumstances, try to provide a wide range of possibilities.

When a teenager is experiencing a powerful emotion, keep in mind that discussing emotions with them won't be as successful. Preventively or after the feeling has subsided, you need to act.

Signs That Your Child May Require Assistance in Learning to Control Their Emotions
All children, particularly younger ones or those facing additional difficulties like a family funeral or other traumatic incident, need assistance and

support from time to time to manage their powerful emotions.

Moreover, pre-teens and teenagers may require assistance if they: appear to make poor judgments as a result of intense emotions, such as frustration; struggle to unwind sufficiently to engage in their hobbies or spend time with family and friends.

Adolescent Emotional Development: Typical Worries

The emotional growth of their teen is something that many parents are curious about. Some question whether it is moving too quickly or too slowly. Others worry about potential drug usage, elevated stress, anxiety, or sadness. There are many different feelings that teenagers (and adults!) might experience, and moodiness occasionally occurs. Teenagers have a wide variety of fast-shifting emotions, which we must be aware of. Most of these highs and lows are typical of their developmental stage and are brought on by how their brains are changing. Yet, parents need to understand what is typical and when it's appropriate to talk to children about their emotions.

There may be instances when it's difficult to tell if your teenagers are experiencing typical growing pains or if there's something more going on. Yet because you are the one who knows your kid the best, it's critical to believe your gut.

Physical Development Is Either Too Quick Or Too Slow.
The emotional development of adolescence can be impacted by puberty progression. Teenagers who mature faster or slower than their peers could be subjected to greater bullying and taunting, and they might also engage in riskier sexual behavior. Their issues with self-esteem or body image could be problematic. Everybody has had moments when they have doubts about their bodies, but if your teen seems obsessive or is struggling to cope with their appearance, think about getting them treatment. Help children

identify bullying and learn how to stop it by providing them with guidance.

Attractions and Romantic Relationships
Expressing one's sexuality and starting to demonstrate an interest in dating are normal teenage experiences. From the first crush to the first breakup, parents are frequently worried about the emotional toll partnerships may take as well as potential medical concerns. Teenagers frequently feel attracted to others and go through a variety of feelings that go along with that. Parents must talk to their children about healthy relationships, consent, and what's suitable and inappropriate.

Teens can get helpful assistance from us as they navigate their sexual and romantic interactions. We must intervene and seek out professional assistance if we believe or see our teenagers involved in relationships that may be physically or emotionally harmful. For instance, there could be cause for alarm if one partner in a relationship starts to be possessive or jealous. Are they attempting to stop the other from going out with friends? control the other person's free time? require access to the other person's phone? To successfully decide if and when you need to get involved, don't be hesitant to ask questions.

Issues with Emotional Expression

Adolescents can be dealing with problems that they don't want to talk about with us. Some teenagers may at times come across as distant and uncommunicative due to their demand for solitude and independence. They might retreat more if we exert too much pressure. If we give them too much room, we might be concerned that they'll wander off. As they navigate various problems and circumstances, we must learn to strike a balance by providing them with solitude, love, and support.

Be the kind of parent that teenagers want to talk to by being a good listener, refraining from judgment or reaction, and encouraging them to find solutions for themselves. A peaceful, cozy, and private discussion can be set up by being attentive to the time and location we choose to have crucial conversations. Depending on the circumstances, it's possible that your teen feels more at ease speaking to someone else than you. Tell them it's ok to discuss it with a trusted friend or relative.

The Psychological Cost of Stress

Teenagers deal with a lot of strain. These might include juggling new obligations and managing classmates and school. Stress is to be expected and even normal. Parents must teach their children a variety of good coping mechanisms so that they can deal with issues, maintain their health, and regulate their emotions. We need to set an example of how to properly manage stress in healthy ways. You should be aware that many of the bad habits our teenagers develop are an effort to cope with stress. At times, tension can seem excessive. We must encourage our teenagers to seek help if they feel they can't handle the stress they are under.

When Our Concerns Become Too Much To Handle

It might not always be clear whether your adolescent is experiencing typical growing pains or if there is something more going on. Yet since you are the one who knows your kid the best, you must believe your gut. Do not be afraid to seek professional assistance if you believe there to be a serious issue or if your teen's feelings seem strong or persistent despite your attempts to address them. Refer young people seeking assistance to medical practitioners, school counselors, or mental health specialists. Make sure your teenagers understand how much they deserve to feel well on the inside.

Chapter 4

Educating Preteens and Teenagers on Emotional Regulation

The teenage years can be a difficult emotional journey filled with many obstacles. There may be some irritability. We anticipate more intense feelings. The strongest kind of protection for youngsters is always their parents' constant presence. Nonetheless, the foundation of security in uncertain times is parental love and constancy.

Parents frequently wonder why their preteens act up over "nothing" or why their teenagers are so disrespectful and "in your face." Adolescent emotions range widely. They can change swiftly from pouting to losing it, from joy to sadness, from giddiness to melancholy, and from sourness to severe rage. So how does a parent assist a teen in handling their emotions well?

Given their raging hormones, a brain still developing, academic stresses, peer pressure, culturally conflicted signals, and computer addiction teaching emotional intelligence to kids is a huge task. With so many difficulties, it's understandable why teenagers struggle with self-control.

Parental responses are a major teaching tool for teen self-regulation and emotional control. All parents want their kids to be polite, develop emotional maturity, and use the healthy emotional expression. Everyone wants to see a successful, caring, responsible, and happy adult as the final product. Many parents, however, demand that their children acquire emotional self-control without providing them with the foundational tools. Emotional development is a journey rather than a destination.

We miss the fact that emotional self-control is a learned skill that is modeled and developed throughout thousands of contacts with parents and caregivers from infancy through adolescence and into young adulthood. Our teenagers ought to wear a sign that reads "Work in Progress" across their chests.

Teenagers don't just magically learn how to manage their emotions one day. It takes practice to control your emotions. Managing one's emotions but still knowing how to express them is a challenging and complex ability. Teenagers too require assistance, compassion, and direction. Your child requires the perfect input so they may naturally acquire self-control, much like plants need the right amount of sunlight, water, nutrients, and good soil to grow well.

Essentials for Your Adolescent to Have a Healthy Emotional Life

For our preteens and adolescents to mature emotionally, there are a few constant components required. By acting as parents, we may establish the conditions that will enable a child to thrive through and through adolescence, much like providing a plant with the best possible environment. To help our kids, preteens, and teens learn emotional self-control, here are some essential things we may provide them:

1. A peaceful, objective mirror for the child's emotions that allows the kid or teen to see clearly and comprehend what they're feeling
2. For the teen to process their experiences and emotions, there must be safety, comprehension, and empathy.
3. Provide clear guidelines that are congruent with their developmental stage.
4. Demonstration of positive emotional expression
5. Teens receive tender assistance to learn how to express their feelings in appropriate ways
6. An awareness of their influence on other people

Before responding to the teen's behaviors, parents must take the time to pay attention to their own internal experiences and feelings. Only then can they give these elements. The secret is to gather your composure and rediscover your love for the teen before answering. The catch is that parents must possess the emotional intelligence to pull this off!

Acting as A Role Model for Teens

Children develop emotional intelligence through observing and experiencing their primary caregivers' caring, empathetic, yet firm responses. The best approach for parents to give their children everything on the above list is by taking responsibility for their mental health and by being honest, or by acknowledging that we are only human (not perfect, not superheroes). This entails embracing our flaws and being compassionate with ourselves when we make a mistake. For us to be able to control our intense emotions, taking care of ourselves is essential. Effective modeling also includes saying sorry and making amends when we mess up and yell (remember, we're human).

We offer our kids the biggest boost in emotional intelligence by leading by example and having a genuine and caring relationship with ourselves.

Here are some tips to help you develop a great relationship with your emotional self as well as some suggestions for how to aid your preteen or adolescent as they discover their emotional nature. So, kids will naturally acquire emotional maturity.

How to Have a Real Connection with Your Feelings and Your Teen!
Firstly, refrain from judging your own or your teen's feelings.

We compare and judge when we categorize feelings as being either good or terrible, positive or negative. But, we all experience emotions, which are merely energies in motion that serve to orient us toward our True North. We frequently describe a behavior or feeling as "bad" when we or our teen displays it (for example, when one of us has an emotional outburst). Also, when we do this, we frequently overreact in a knee-jerk manner and attempt to control or alter the mood or behavior. Because of this, our teen frequently explodes or suppresses their feelings instead of developing emotional resilience. (Without exercise, we cannot strengthen our emotional muscles.)

What if, in contrast, we thought of behavior as merely communication and emotion as a compass? How does our perspective about our teens and ourselves change now? Indeed, we can take a step back and speak with more kindness. To respond to what we or our kid needs, rather than only attempting to stop the emotion or alter or correct the behavior, we are now looking to understand. This type of activity teaches the child to be in control of their own emotions while providing them with the chance to train and strengthen their emotional muscles.

Secondly, recognize and attend to your own emotions before addressing those of your preteen or adolescent.

Before reacting to your teen, give it a minute or a day. They can use this time to reflect, feel, settle down, and stew. An advantage is that you can teach your preteen or adolescent how to relax by doing it yourself!

One of the most important factors in parenting well is parental self-regulation. This self-awareness and self-comfort are especially important throughout the difficult teenage years.

Thirdly, reflect your teen's or preteen's feelings accurately.

Their ability to understand their emotional experience will increase the more correctly we can reflect their emotions. They don't get to experience, own, or deal with their feelings when we react since the focus shifts to how we're feeling and how upset we are, rather than how they are experiencing.

The teen will be able to comprehend and apply the following teachings more effectively with an accurate mirror:

Lesson 1: All emotions are valid, and I can express and manage them;

Lesson 2: I'm responsible for my feelings;

Lesson 3: Feelings are fleeting and go away when acknowledged;

LESSON 4: Feelings guide me to take better care of myself;

Lesson 5: Others are impacted by my actions.

Fourthly, empathize with their emotions

You may have noticed that while sentiments that are affirmed dissipate, feelings that go ignored tend to accumulate until they explode—often at inconvenient moments. Creating a safe space for your preteen or teen to experience emotions, especially strong emotions, allows your child a chance to practice controlling and refocusing emotions under your guidance in healthy and appropriate ways. The key to navigating the intense emotions of adolescence is to give, teach, and model empathy. And sometimes, it's crucial to simply share in their laughter.

Fifthly, explain what you see and how their actions make you feel.

Share your views with kids and teenagers without passing judgment. What expression do they have? (Angry, pleased, sad, etc.) What are they saying with their body language? (Fist clenched, arms crossed, etc.) How does their voice sound? (Dejected, thrilled, etc.) You can assist the kid or adolescent in making the connection between what you observe and how it affects their body and their relationships by articulating what you see in detail.

A preteen or teen may claim to be fine yet act otherwise based on their body language. It's critical to let them know that what they are saying and what you observe don't match up in this situation. Your preteen or teen can check in with their internal experience and own an emotion they may have been avoiding when you point out this mismatch. Also, it opens up the possibility of a conversation, which gives you the chance to mentor.

Sometimes a teen only has to accept their sentiments to move on. They occasionally need to understand our reactions to their actions. For illustration, we could remark, "Wow! I feel this incredibly powerful force approaching me. I feel like backing away from it." Or "I'm interested in hearing your opinion. When you're ready to speak to me politely and quit screaming, I'll be in the kitchen." Alternatively, "I value what you have to say, but it seems like you might use a moment to unwind before our conversation."

We can unwind by keeping in mind that we're all only human, including our preteens and teens, and that reaching emotional maturity is a journey of growth, not an endpoint. The relationships we have with our spouse, our teen, our neighbors, and the rest of the world, as well as with ourselves (including our emotions), are what we should concentrate on.

Have patience with yourself. Keep your preteen or teen in the center of your love. Respond to your teen from a firm and grounded place while remaining aware of your own experience. These parental reactions will benefit both you and your adolescent greatly, including fostering a caring and supportive connection.

Chapter 5

How to Navigate the Difficulties That Come with Adolescence

Children go through several changes at this time as they transition from childhood to adulthood. Children are particularly vulnerable during this time because they may encounter a variety of adolescent issues, such as unhealthy habits that could have serious consequences down the road. It can be challenging for parents to connect with their children during this time due to concerns about typical adolescent behavior.

Teenagers are impacted by a wide range of circumstances, including puberty-related physical, emotional, cognitive, and social changes. The bodily changes frequently elicit curiosity and worry and lower self-esteem. Their desire for independence is fueled by social causes. Adolescents think more abstractly and make complex decisions as a result of frontal lobe brain changes. Teenagers experience emotional changes frequently as a result of hormonal changes brought on by puberty.

For either kids or parents, adolescence is rarely an easy period. At this age, the only way to handle wants and issues is to be aware of them and prepared to deal with them. Conflicts between parents and their children that lead to unstable and uneasy feelings are linearly related to pubertal maturity. Your child could become more responsible and social if they comprehend and deal with these disputes positively.

This is our list of the issues that affect teens the most frequently, along with solutions.

1. Physical modifications

Changes in a teen's hormone levels result in physical changes.

- It can initially be uncomfortable for females to develop full breasts. Girls could begin to feel self-conscious about their physique.

- The most noticeable change that occurs during adolescence in boys is probably a shift in voice and the development of facial hair.
- One of the biggest issues is acne.
- Teenagers who build muscle might occasionally become overweight.
- The expansion of pubic hair in both boys and girls.
- It becomes clear that there is body odor.
- Girls begin to experience their periods.

Solution

Making your kid aware of these changes is the greatest approach to assist them in getting through this phase.

- Explain that while every adolescent experiences physical change, it is normal.
- Help them adjust to these changes by acknowledging the shift and assisting them in accepting it.
- Provide them with the tools they need to maintain their health and fitness through a balanced diet and regular exercise.

2. Problems and shifts in an emotional state

Your teen's hormones have both physical and psychological effects.

- The period of life between childhood and adulthood is known as adolescence. Adolescents are frequently conflicted about their roles and divided between their obligations as developing adults and their aspirations as youngsters.
- They frequently exhibit excessive emotionality (blame it on the hormones). They can get thrilled, angry, or joyful about almost anything.
- Teenage girls are more prone to sobbing.
- Teenage boys and girls frequently experience mood swings.
- Self-consciousness arises from physical changes.
- Early puberty can even make kids feel strange.
- At this point, feelings of inferiority or superiority could appear.

- Young people first experience sexual desires during their adolescence. Guilt can be sparked by sexual thoughts and feelings.

Solution

An emotional whirlwind might be puberty. Moreover, it is typical. Here's how you can support your adolescent in navigating these emotional issues.

- Help them take care of themselves. Remind your teenagers that it's okay for them to feel how they do.
- Urge them to exercise since it keeps their serotonin levels—which produce positive emotions and happiness—high.
- Let them speak. Avoid offering them advice when they are not ready for it and listen to them without passing judgment.
- Discuss your own experiences with puberty with them, or allow them to speak with an older sibling who has also gone through it. It will stress that feeling as they do is acceptable.

- They can better manage their emotions by engaging in creative activities.

3. Behavioral modifications

Intense emotions can cause impulsive conduct, which can be dangerous for both your child and other people. The majority of it is simply teenage behavior that will endure as long as their youth.

- Children gain and practice their independence during adolescence. This may lead to challenging the rules of the parents and defending what they feel is right (seen as stubbornness).
- Teenagers are temperamental, exhausted, and challenging to manage due to significant brain growth.
- Teenage guys' raging hormones may even encourage them to engage in physical altercations. They would also like to hear loud music.
- Adolescents may desire to try new things and take risks as a result of their newly found independence, which can lead to reckless behavior.

- Peer pressure and the desire to "fit in" can occasionally cause people to behave in particular ways or form difficult-to-break habits.
- Your teen's appearance, sense of style, and manner of clothing all change, frequently in ways that you might not like.
- Perhaps your teen hanging around with troubled kids and acclimating to a harmful lifestyle is the most alarming behavior.
- One of the frequent behavioral problems among teenagers is lying. Teenagers may tell lies out of fear or to avoid conflict with their parents.

Solution

Adolescent behavior issues can make parenting challenging. However, keep in mind that it is only a temporary stage and completely normal.

- If you wish to assist your child with behavioral challenges, you must first earn their trust. Interact with them and pay attention to what they have to say. Avoid passing judgment or offering criticism because doing so might make their conduct worse.

- Tell them you adore them for who they are. Urge them to stay true to themselves and avoid adopting a personality only to win over others.
- Keep in mind that your adolescent child needs your help and is not entirely independent in handling their emotions. Assist them by explaining what you do when you're depressed, enraged, jealous, etc. They can use those remedies to resolve their emotional problems.
- If you notice them mixing with the wrong crowd, you will need to step in and stop it. Keep in mind that teenagers are impressionable and might not take criticism well.

4. Addiction to drugs and alcohol

Adolescents are impressionable and easily influenced, making them particularly susceptible. One of the largest issues facing parents of teenagers everywhere is substance misuse.

- Teenagers who smoke, drink, or use drugs are often influenced by their peers, which is one of the major motivators.
- Most teenagers try smoking or drinking before they are old enough to do so due to their propensity for taking risks.
- If left unchecked, anything that could initially be a "thrill" can develop into a habit.
- Role models for your teen can include people who smoke or drink alcohol at home.
- Teenagers who smoke or drink may do so because of low self-esteem or a desire to fit in.
- It may become more tempting to use illegal substances if they are readily available, such as cigarettes, alcohol, narcotics, and anabolic steroids.

Solution
- Observe your child's actions. Be on the lookout for unpredictable behavior as well

as adjustments to their eating, sleep, and mood.

- Do not snoop on them or make any false accusations against them. Promote open communication and honesty with them. As you address the issue with them, express your worries to them.
- The physicians can ask private inquiries to find out if your child is abusing any drugs if they are unwilling to speak with you. Don't go as far as a drug test because that can come off as hostile and threatening to the child.
- Get your teen the required care if it's needed.

5. Problems with school

Fashion, friends, and parties aren't the only things the high school has to offer. The educational schedules of children are likewise very full.

The quest for independence that adolescents experience during a crucial period of brain development makes academics difficult for them frequently. Teenagers frequently desire to be self-sufficient and do not want their parents to constantly remind them to finish their homework. Their brain is evolving in such a way that it enables them to move from concrete to abstract thinking, which frequently leads them to make bad academic decisions. Unfortunately, some adolescents don't place a high premium on their academics. Adolescents frequently form their own set of ideals.

- Your adolescent may get irritable under pressure to succeed academically and gain college admission.
- It can be challenging to balance extracurricular activities, schoolwork, and household duties (all required for college admissions).
- The pressure will increase if there are distractions at school that lead to low academic achievement.

Solution

- Encourage your youngster to pursue his or her dreams of attending college because that is what they require.
- To give kids more time to work on their schoolwork when necessary, you could reduce their home duties.
- Exercise and proper nutrition can provide kids with the stamina and strength they need to get through the demanding high school years.
- Cut back on a few tasks if you think your adolescent is becoming overburdened by his daily obligations because adolescents still lack adult-level lung capacity and exhaust more quickly than adults do.

6. Health Issues

Both emotionally and physiologically, adolescents are weak. They are more vulnerable to illnesses without access to healthy food and medical care.

- Teens frequently switch between activities, which leaves them with little time to adequately eat or rest. They cannot obtain the necessary nourishment because of their unhealthy eating habits.

- Particularly in girls, eating disorders can be brought on by body consciousness. Disorders like bulimia or anorexia can occur in adolescent girls who are concerned about their weight and appearance.
- In young children, stress can also cause appetite loss and disrupted sleep.
- Obesity may also be caused by unhealthy eating patterns and a sedentary lifestyle, which is frequently the case when your child consumes a lot of sodas and fast meals that are high in empty calories.

Solution

To maintain a healthy lifestyle during adolescence, parental supervision can assist reduce health issues. Set an example by eating well, exercising regularly, and getting enough sleep for your kids.

- Don't forget to feed them nutritious food. A balanced diet should be provided.

- You can assist them to deal with any potential illnesses by being there for them both physically and emotionally.

7. Emotional difficulties

According to research, over half of all mental health illnesses in adults start when a person is 14 years old. Depression has a role in one-third of adolescent suicides. Get immediate professional assistance for your child if they are very grumpy, not eating, or not sleeping at all.

Anxiety and mood disorders are the two most prevalent mental health conditions seen in adolescents. This age group is prone to social anxieties and panic attacks. The likelihood of developing depressive disorders may be higher in girls than in boys.

- Teens may struggle with confidence or difficulties with their worth. Many times, one's looks and acceptance of one's body—including one's skin tone, beauty, and figure—cause one to feel inferior or superior.

- Also demotivating them include poor academic achievement and low Intelligence. People grow to believe that they are unworthy of happiness.
- One of the frequent mental health issues that adolescents experience is depression.
- The pressure and stress of adolescence can cause anxiety-related problems, and mood swings might result in conduct disorder or oppositional defiant disorder.
- Due to the adolescent's negative self-image and desire to improve their appearance in any way, eating disorders are also psychosomatic.

Solution

Temper tantrums and moodiness are common in adolescent males and girls, but they aren't always what they appear. It can be difficult and requires a trained eye to recognize signs of psychological issues in adolescents.

- In most cases, discussing the issues and leading a healthy lifestyle can stop depression from starting.

- You should step in and, if necessary, seek professional assistance if your child is too irritable and pessimistic.
- Your adolescent child might occasionally be content elsewhere but miserable at home. To find out if other students are irritable and confused at school, ask the child's instructors and friends. They should be worried if they are.
- Rejecting their emotions could make matters worse, so avoid doing so.
- Get them talking to you by encouraging it. Talk to them about this if you want to. Talk to your child in the car instead of face-to-face if you fear they won't take it well. This will reduce the likelihood of an argument.

8. Dating and relationship-related social issues

At puberty, a person first feels attracted to the opposite sex. They begin to grow their reproductive or sexual organs during adolescence. Teenagers naturally feel uncomfortable in social interactions at such a sensitive age.

- Teenagers desire their own unique identities. In the home or outside, they frequently emulate positive role models.
- Also, adolescents begin to challenge their perspectives on various issues and consider what is "good" and "wrong."
- To comprehend and feel at ease with their sexuality, they need time.
- Both boys and girls start having "strange" feelings toward the opposite sex and may not know how to deal with them. Now that they are dating, they begin.
- Your adolescent could feel awkward discussing it with you and rely on the scant or inaccurate knowledge they have of it.
- A teenager's social life should also include competition. Your youngster can engage in endless competition with her peers. Their competitive spirit conveys a lot about how they view themselves, whether they have a high or low sense of self.

- Adolescents could feel guilty for having sex-related thoughts and sensations because they may perceive them as improper.
- They seem to be busy communicating with pals on social media sites, on their phones, and outside during this time, which results in an expansion of their social circle.

Solution

Adolescent social issues can be handled in the following ways:

- It's possible that your kid doesn't feel comfortable talking to you about dating, romance, or sexual activity. Avoid adding to your child's discomfort.When speaking about the topic, be assured and logical.
- If it seems like your child spends more time outside than inside with you. Embrace the fact that your teenagers are exploring a brand-new universe. Let them know that you are available for them at any time.

- They might feel more at ease if you talk about your dating and social life experiences in class.

9. STIs and impromptu pregnancies about sexual health

Teenagers' new sentiments and want to experiment with their bodies are fueled by the development of secondary sexual traits during adolescence.

- Adolescence is the time when teens have their first kiss, private dance with their "boyfriend" or "girlfriend," and have covert make-out sessions.
- Teenagers could start acting sexually before they're ready if they lack sufficient coaching. Unwanted pregnancy may be the outcome of this. The biggest threat that teenage girls confront is unwanted pregnancy.
- Having intercourse without protection increases the risk of contracting HIV and other STDs.

Solution

- Talk to your kids about sexuality and reproduction because they may already be studying it in school. Making sure they recognize the value of safe sex is your responsibility as a parent.
- Teenagers may act impulsively due to hormonal changes in their bodies. Even though they might not like it, it's crucial to have a conversation with your teen about the dangers of unprotected sex and how it might alter their life.
- Adolescent STIs and early pregnancies cannot be prevented without increased awareness.

10.Internet addiction

We now connect differently thanks to social media. The teenage way of life has been most impacted.

- Your teenager might appear to be on the phone, texting, talking, or just playing for hours. Internet-dependent teenagers typically have fewer friends and less of an active social life. They enjoy living by themselves and spending a lot of time online.

- An unhealthy and sedentary lifestyle is the outcome of their reduced physical activity due to addiction to the internet.
- Poor academic achievement is a result of internet addiction.

Solution

- If your child spends a lot of time in front of the computer, do not automatically assume that they are addicted to the internet. In contrast to web surfing, they may be using the machine for more useful activities.
- Give the Internet your unwavering support. They'll get more adamant as a result. As an alternative, discuss your worries with them and assist them with tasks that do not use computers.
- You could impose restrictions on your teen, but keep in mind that they are no longer children and might not appreciate it.

- The ability to make wise decisions may also be lacking in them at the same time. Thus, as a parent, you should guide kids but never make decisions for them.
- Sign them up for pursuits that promote social interaction. Encourage them to spend less time on the computer by organizing family activities.
- Everyone at home should be subject to some online guidelines and limitations. Don't use your phone more than a few hours a day, and stay away from the bedroom as it may interfere with your sleep.

11. Violent behavior and aggression

Boy adolescent aggression is particularly problematic. The muscles, height, and manly voice of young boys begin to develop.

Moreover, they have volatile personalities, are prone to vulnerability, and are easily offended.

- Teenage boys may engage in physical altercations at school.

- Worst still, they might start bullying others, which is a serious issue that both adolescent males and girls deal with.
- Males are more likely to be drawn to aggressive behavior, violence, and bad company.
- They might be readily persuaded to own or employ a weapon or a firearm. Violence committed on the spur of the moment has the potential to be fatal.
- Adolescent girls frequently experience partner abuse or aggressiveness.

Solution

Kids frequently mimic what they observe at home. Aggression, violence, and other disorders connected to adolescence can be reduced with the following treatments.

- Instill kindness and consideration in your children.
- They can learn to be less violent by being nurtured in the family.
- To reduce violence, restrict early access to alcohol and weapons.

- Show kids the value of kindness and impart life skills.
- Be their role model and guide them.

You Can Assist When You Are Aware

In shaping their children's behavior, parents are quite influential. You can have a good effect by teaching your teen about potential issues and how to solve them. As opposed to passing judgment or being impolite to them, understanding their sentiments and making recommendations can help to reduce confrontations.

It may be easier for your child to refrain from poor behavior and drug usage if you establish clear restrictions for them. You may encourage your child to talk to you about their problems and ask for your assistance by developing open and friendly communication with them.

Chapter 6

Developing Positive Relationships with Your Teens

For both children and parents, adolescence is a confusing and challenging time. The behaviors and habits your adolescent child picks up now could have a long-term impact on their personality and character. Yet, these are crucial years for character development.

These days, a lot of parents experience frustration. Your relationship with your formerly obedient child may seem to be deteriorating if there are frequent attitude conflicts. The reality is that your teenagers are probably simply trying to figure out who they are and how far they can go in terms of their morals, as well as how much they can tolerate in both themselves and others.

You and your child can manage a good relationship via mutual respect and affection in a variety of methods that don't need to be complicated. Once you adjust to the fact that your child is now a young adult, all it takes is for you to maintain your composure and practice patience.

Recognize Your Anxiety

We can all relate to the confusion and changes that teenagers must deal with because we were once that age. We provide them with a release valve and a source of consolation when we try to comprehend their angst. Most of the time, you'll discover that you can identify with their annoyances and that you might perhaps provide them with helpful suggestions.

Make Use of Your Own Experiences

Teenagers are at a special phase of life where they are attempting to learn more about themselves, their environment, and society. Due to their growing rebellious nature, this could land them in legal problems.

Being quick to judge your child in such a circumstance is the absolute last thing you should do. Instead, put yourself in their position; reflect on your own experiences as a young person and the coping mechanisms you used. Give your youngster the same consoling words that you required as an adolescent.

A Friend in Technology

Teenagers now have far more information available to them than any of us did while we were growing up thanks to the internet. Facebook, Twitter, Instagram, and other social media sites play crucial parts in your teen's life and are useful tools for monitoring your teen's whereabouts and social behavior. Build greater connections with your teen by learning to communicate with them using the same tools, the same language, and the same media.

Respect Is Earned Through Mutual Regard

Nothing is more offensive to parents than a disobedient child. Respect is a two-way street, so put aside your parental pride and keep in mind that this will help keep your family happy and healthy. Simple actions like respecting your adolescent's privacy, treating them like young adults, and acknowledging their decisions can go a long way toward fostering respect between you and your adolescent.

Don't panic.
Spend a few seconds each time to remind yourself to remain composed. Although your adolescent's impolite behavior can be upsetting, escalating the situation with threats and arguments will only make things worse. Consider what your youngster might have been attempting to say as an adult and stand back. Consider strategies to help them communicate more clearly, for instance, if they may have had a point they were unable to make themselves clear about. Choose to continue the talk later, once you are more composed if you find yourself losing your cool.

Demonstrate An Interest in Their Interests
Taking an active interest in their children's activities and getting to know their interests and

hobbies is crucial for parents. The simplest approach to show your adolescent that you care is to do this. It will also enable you and your adolescent to have more conversations together.

Understand Their Friends
Investigate your child's friends in more detail. Improved communication between you and your adolescent can result from their involvement in social activities. Your kids can talk to you about their social lives thanks to this, as a parent. You will also feel more at ease when your teen is out because you will know whether they are hanging out with the correct crowd.

Give Your Teen A Larger Family Role
Housework and home maintenance are only a small part of what it means to be a household member. It fosters an awareness of duty and ownership. Participate with your teen in family talks and treat them like a young adult with mature thoughts. Encourage your adolescent to establish personal rules and make sure they are followed.

Keep speaking

Talk to your adolescent frequently. You might be the ideal outlet for them if they have thoughts they don't want to share with their buddies. Rely on your own adolescent experience once more to provide them with the guidance they require. You might not necessarily need to speak first in some circumstances. It could be that all they need is one that can provide a listening ear.

A Fun Time

Keep in mind that quality overrides quantity when it comes to time spent with your adolescent. It's not necessary to spend every evening with your adolescent, but make sure to schedule time for a special meal or a day out just to relax or partake in their favorite activity. With your adolescent, try out some novel activities like fishing, seeking out culinary treats, or competing in video games. Regardless of age, your child will undoubtedly appreciate the time spent and look forward to further activities.

Relevant Lessons

Recognize that it is only normal for a teenager at this point in their lives to desire to spend more time with their friends. Making an effort to spend time with your child regularly will help you stay informed about what is happening in their lives.

When things become hot, maintain your composure since only by speaking clearly and firmly can you get your point across. You can always reschedule the chat for a time when you feel more composed if you realize that you are too furious to speak clearly. It allows you both more time to think and concentrate on improving your mutual understanding.

Attempt to comprehend what your child enjoys doing and learn more about the friends that your child values. It gives you a better understanding of your child's personality and increases the chances that the two of you will connect.

Chapter 7

Advantages of Positive Teens Parenting

Without a question, as a parent, you have protected your child throughout all of their formative years. Now that they are adolescents, they long for freedom from the authority and the ability to make their own decisions. Planned Parenthood claims that as teenagers, our children become much more independent. This is a typical and natural aspect of growing up. We must maintain our bonds with them at the same level as when they were little, despite their growing independence. Kids continue to require our love, guidance, and enjoyment.

As much as your teen wants to be in charge of his or her own life, you as the parent need to show some level of control and authority. The lack of life experience can prevent a kid from making the best decisions, even though they may believe they are old enough and know everything there is to know. This is related to every parent's worry that their teen will start developing risky habits.

Adolescents often test the limits of their own experiences and boundaries, and they might be particularly vulnerable to peer pressure. Although you can't be present all the time to supervise your teen's behavior, you may serve as an authoritative figure and a trusted friend. The most important thing is to convey to your kid that you are there and that any worries you have are genuine and for their good.

Setting healthy boundaries and building a strong family unit need to communicate that you recognize your adolescent child's independence while maintaining your position as the parent in charge. A healthy, balanced young adult who knows right from wrong, cares about other people, and is proud of themselves and their abilities is what parents hope to raise. While starting throughout adolescence may seem like a daunting task, it is.

Here are five methods to keep your connection with your adolescent healthy and content for both of you:

1. Take time off together

When a youngster turns into an adolescent, hanging out with parents suddenly loses a lot of its appeal. Reinforcing family structure, however, can help a teen feel supported and well-adjusted while also giving them a chance to confide in a parent. To help your teen as they navigate adolescence, you should take any opportunity to let them know you are there.

2. Be an excellent role model

While it is not necessary to be a saint, it is unquestionably beneficial for teenagers to view their parents as role models for appropriate behavior. Be careful how many substances you consume in front of your teenager, especially if you drink too much or smoke a lot, as they are likely to imitate any good habits they observe at home.

3. Define limits

Even if there is a young adult living with you, you are still the primary adult, and your child must understand that you are the one who sets the boundaries. Setting boundaries for your kid calmly and strongly is crucial. A lack of boundaries might cause teenagers to feel dissatisfied with their level of freedom as they enter adulthood.

4. Show deference

Teenagers today are more concerned than ever about criticism and jeer due to the rise of cyberbullying. A sensitive kid may experience taunting as torment. No matter how subtly, don't make fun of your teen, and stay away from insulting words and gestures. When a parent says anything like this, it can lower a teen's self-esteem and make them feel uneasy and uncomfortable at home.

5. Exude concern

Your child needs to know that you love and support them through this difficult time, so make a special lunch for them or send them a message "just because." Take the time to apologize and reaffirm your unwavering love for your teenager if you and they disagree after a disagreement. Stress the importance of the family and the unwavering love it possesses, and encourage your teen to participate in it.

Even though raising a teenager isn't always simple, it's always beneficial to make an effort to build a solid bond that values mutual respect and affection. A parent's counsel and support are essential as their child navigates the challenges of adolescence, even though every teenager is unique.